Norman Rockwell

Postcard Book

Running Press
Philadelphia, Pennsylvania

Canadian representatives: General Publishing Co., Ltd.,
30 Lesmill Road, Don Mills, Ontario M3B 2T6.

International representatives: Worldwide Media Services,
Inc., 115 East 23rd Street, New York, NY 10010.

9   8   7   6   5   4   3
Digit on right indicates the number of this printing.

ISBN 0-89471-554-2 (Paper)
Cover design by Toby Schmidt
Cover illustration: *Freedom from Want* by Norman Rockwell.
Collection of The Norman Rockwell Museum at
Stockbridge, Massachusetts.
Copyright © 1943 Estate of Norman Rockwell,
reproduced by permission.

Back cover illustration: *Triple Self-Portrait* by Norman
Rockwell. Cover for *The Saturday Evening Post*, February 13,
1960. Collection of The Norman Rockwell Museum at
Stockbridge, Massachusetts.
Copyright © 1960 Estate of Norman Rockwell,
reproduced by permission.
Spine illustration (detail): *After the Prom* by Norman Rockwell.
Cover for *The Saturday Evening Post*, May 25, 1957.
Copyright © 1957 Estate of Norman Rockwell,
reproduced by permission.
Illustrations and captions copyright © 1987
Estate of Norman Rockwell, reproduced and reprinted
by permission of the Estate of Norman Rockwell.

Typography by Today's Graphics, Philadelphia, PA.
Printed and bound in Hong Kong by Leefung Asco Ltd.

This book can be ordered by mail from the publisher.
Please include $1.00 postage and handling for each copy.
But try your bookstore first!
Running Press Book Publishers
125 South 22 Street, Philadelphia, Pennsylvania 19103

Freedom from Fear by Norman Rockwell. Rockwell's "Four Freedoms" series, inspired by President Roosevelt's Four Freedoms Proclamation, was published in *The Saturday Evening Post* in 1943. Collection of The Norman Rockwell Museum at Stockbridge, MA. Copyright © 1943 Estate of Norman Rockwell, reproduced by permission.

Norman Rockwell Postcard Book © 1987 by Running Press Book Publishers

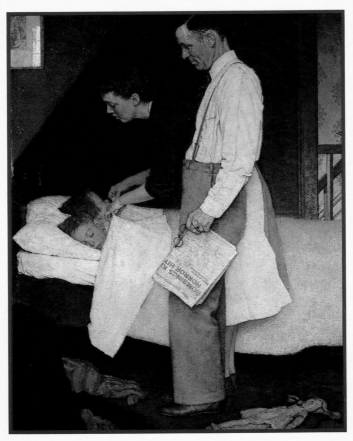

Norman Rockwell

Freedom from Fear

After the Prom by Norman Rockwell. Cover for *The Saturday Evening Post*, May 25, 1957. "I call this my chinless picture....I had intended to paint a warm, pleasant picture...But then I was overcome with an irresistible impulse to caricature." —Norman Rockwell. Copyright © 1957 Estate of Norman Rockwell, reprinted by permission of the Estate of Norman Rockwell. Photo courtesy of The Norman Rockwell Museum at Stockbridge, MA.

Norman Rockwell Postcard Book © 1987 by Running Press Book Publishers

Norman Rockwell

After the Prom

Going and Coming by Norman Rockwell. Cover for *The Saturday Evening Post*, August 30, 1947. "This was the first of the two-part *Post* covers and I'm kind of proud I painted it." —Norman Rockwell. Collection of The Norman Rockwell Museum at Stockbridge, MA. Copyright © 1947 Estate of Norman Rockwell, reproduced by permission.

Norman Rockwell Postcard Book © 1987 by Running Press Book Publishers

Norman Rockwell

Going and Coming

Christmas Trio by Norman Rockwell. Cover for *The Saturday Evening Post*, December 8, 1923. "Most of my early covers were of kids... pictures reflecting a nostalgia for nineteenth-century rural America..." —Norman Rockwell. Collection of The Norman Rockwell Museum at Stockbridge, MA. Copyright © 1923 Estate of Norman Rockwell, reproduced by permission.

Norman Rockwell Postcard Book © 1987 by Running Press Book Publishers

Norman Rockwell

Christmas Trio

Art Critic by Norman Rockwell. Cover for *The Saturday Evening Post*, April 16, 1955. "I could not determine what the woman in the portrait should look like . . . And everyone who came into the studio . . . had a different opinion. I don't remember how many sketches I made of the woman; at least twenty." —Norman Rockwell. Copyright © 1955 Estate of Norman Rockwell, reprinted by permission of the Estate of Norman Rockwell. Photo courtesy of The Norman Rockwell Museum at Stockbridge, MA.

Norman Rockwell Postcard Book © 1987 by Running Press Book Publishers

Norman Rockwell

Art Critic

Before the Shot by Norman Rockwell. Cover for *The Saturday Evening Post*, March 15, 1958. "I guess everyone has sat at one time or another in a doctor's office and examined his diplomas, wondering how good a doctor he was…" —Norman Rockwell. Copyright © 1958 Estate of Norman Rockwell, reprinted by permission of the Estate of Norman Rockwell. Photo courtesy of The Norman Rockwell Museum at Stockbridge, MA.

Norman Rockwell Postcard Book © 1987 by Running Press Book Publishers

Norman Rockwell

Before the Shot

Shuffleton's Barbershop by Norman Rockwell. Cover for *The Saturday Evening Post*, April 29, 1950. "...almost everyone had lived in the town all his life and had known one another since childhood and...there could be little pretension...there was a great neighborliness." —Norman Rockwell. Copyright © 1950 Estate of Norman Rockwell, reprinted by permission of the Estate of Norman Rockwell. Photo courtesy of The Norman Rockwell Museum at Stockbridge, MA.

Norman Rockwell Postcard Book © 1987 by Running Press Book Publishers

Norman Rockwell

Shuffleton's Barbershop

Spring Flowers by Norman Rockwell. Interior illustration for *McCall's Magazine*, May, 1969. "...after a while I realized that I just didn't see things as the modern artists did. I liked...the wild way they used color. But I knew I could never paint that way." —Norman Rockwell. Collection of The Norman Rockwell Museum at Stockbridge, MA. Copyright © 1969 Estate of Norman Rockwell, reproduced by permission.

Norman Rockwell Postcard Book © 1987 by Running Press Book Publishers

Norman
Rockwell

Spring Flowers

The Discovery by Norman Rockwell. Cover for *The Saturday Evening Post*, December 29, 1956. "I'd tacked a false beard on my easel and was trying to paint it so that every hair would look real...After a while...I pulled some hair out of the beard and stuck it in the wet paint on the canvas." —Norman Rockwell. Collection of The Norman Rockwell Museum at Stockbridge, MA. Copyright © 1956 Estate of Norman Rockwell, reproduced by permission.

Norman Rockwell Postcard Book © 1987 by Running Press Book Publishers

Norman
Rockwell

The Discovery

Freedom from Want by Norman Rockwell. The Treasury Department's national tour of this painting and the other three in Rockwell's "Four Freedoms" series was responsible for the sale of $132 million in war bonds during World War II. Collection of The Norman Rockwell Museum at Stockbridge, MA. Copyright © 1943 Estate of Norman Rockwell, reproduced by permission.

Norman Rockwell Postcard Book © 1987 by Running Press Book Publishers

Norman Rockwell

Freedom from Want

Norman Rockwell Postcard Book © 1987 by Running Press Book Publishers

Norman
Rockwell

Sick Puppy

Day in the Life of a Little Girl by Norman Rockwell. Cover for *The Saturday Evening Post*, August 30, 1952. "I prefer to be called an illustrator. But ... *Post* covers are independent, storytelling pictures; they don't 'illustrate' anything." —Norman Rockwell. Collection of The Norman Rockwell Museum at Stockbridge, MA. Copyright © 1952 Estate of Norman Rockwell, reproduced by permission.

Norman Rockwell Postcard Book © 1987 by Running Press Book Publishers

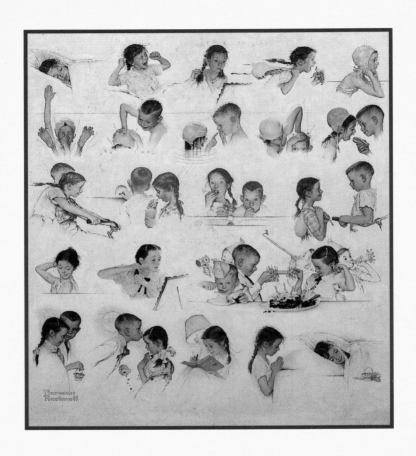

Norman Rockwell

Day in the Life of a Little Girl

Girl at Mirror by Norman Rockwell. Cover for *The Saturday Evening Post*, March 6, 1954. "The model, Mary Whalen,... was the best little-girl model I ever had. She could assume any expression I requested: sad, merry, joyful, wistful, disdainful." —Norman Rockwell. Collection of The Norman Rockwell Museum at Stockbridge, MA. Copyright © 1954 Estate of Norman Rockwell, reproduced by permission.

Norman Rockwell Postcard Book © 1987 by Running Press Book Publishers

Norman Rockwell

Girl at Mirror

Saying Grace by Norman Rockwell. Cover for *The Saturday Evening Post*, November 24, 1951. "If you actually saw such a scene in a railroad station, some of the people ... would have been respectful, some indifferent ... The picture is not absolutely true to life; it's not a photograph of an actual scene but the scene as I *saw* it." —Norman Rockwell. Copyright © 1951 Estate of Norman Rockwell, reprinted by permission of the Estate of Norman Rockwell. Photo courtesy of The Norman Rockwell Museum at Stockbridge, MA.

Norman Rockwell Postcard Book © 1987 by Running Press Book Publishers

Norman Rockwell

Saying Grace

Girl with Black Eye by Norman Rockwell. Cover for *The Saturday Evening Post*, May 23, 1953. "I said I'd pay $5.00 to the bearer of a ripe black eye … Then the wire services picked up the story. And all of a sudden I was deluged with black eyes." —Norman Rockwell. Copyright © 1953 Estate of Norman Rockwell, reprinted by permission of the Estate of Norman Rockwell. Photo courtesy of The Norman Rockwell Museum at Stockbridge, MA.

Norman Rockwell Postcard Book © 1987 by Running Press Book Publishers

Norman Rockwell

Girl with Black Eye

Triple Self-Portrait by Norman Rockwell. Cover for *The Saturday Evening Post*, February 13, 1960. "I like to think that each time people look at one of my covers, they will see something new, something they had not noticed before, which will give the cover an added meaning." —Norman Rockwell. Collection of The Norman Rockwell Museum at Stockbridge, MA. Copyright © 1960 Estate of Norman Rockwell, reproduced by permission.

Norman Rockwell

Triple Self-Portrait

Christmas Homecoming by Norman Rockwell. Cover for *The Saturday Evening Post*, December 25, 1948. Norman Rockwell (at right) and his wife, Mary, welcome their eldest son. The Rockwells' two younger sons also appear here, as does the artist Grandma Moses and other neighbors. Collection of The Norman Rockwell Museum at Stockbridge, MA. Copyright © 1948 Estate of Norman Rockwell, reproduced by permission.

Norman Rockwell Postcard Book © 1987 by Running Press Book Publishers

Norman
Rockwell

Christmas Homecoming

The Runaway by Norman Rockwell. Cover for *The Saturday Evening Post*, September 20, 1958. "I ran away from home when I was a kid in Mamaroneck and mooned around the shore ... Pretty soon it began to get dark and a cold wind sprang up and moaned in the trees. So I went home." —Norman Rockwell. Collection of The Norman Rockwell Museum at Stockbridge, MA. Copyright © 1958 Estate of Norman Rockwell, reproduced by permission.

Norman Rockwell

The Runaway

Day in the Life of a Little Boy by Norman Rockwell. Cover for *The Saturday Evening Post*, May 24, 1952. "Selecting the right models is extremely important; I tell the story through the characters." —Norman Rockwell. Copyright © 1952 Estate of Norman Rockwell, reprinted by permission of the Estate of Norman Rockwell. Photo courtesy of The Norman Rockwell Museum at Stockbridge, MA.

Norman Rockwell Postcard Book © 1987 by Running Press Book Publishers

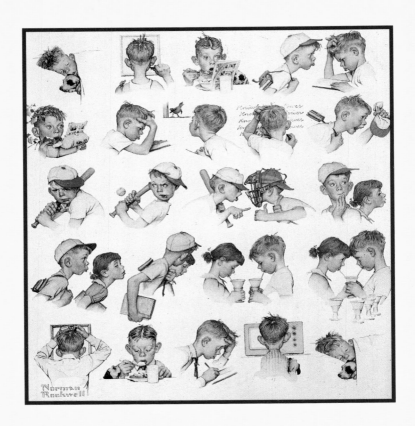

Norman Rockwell

Day in the Life of a Little Boy

Prom Dress by Norman Rockwell. Cover for *The Saturday Evening Post*, March 9, 1949. "...whenever possible, I like to visit and photograph or make sketches of the actual setting of a cover. The room in this cover is an exact reproduction of the model's own room..." —Norman Rockwell. Copyright © 1949 Estate of Norman Rockwell, reprinted by permission of the Estate of Norman Rockwell. Photo courtesy of The Norman Rockwell Museum at Stockbridge, MA.

Norman Rockwell Postcard Book © 1987 by Running Press Book Publishers

Norman Rockwell

Prom Dress

The Optician by Norman Rockwell. Cover for *The Saturday Evening Post*, May 19, 1956. "The cover … must not require an explanation or caption to be understood; it must have an instantaneous impact…" —Norman Rockwell. Copyright © 1956 Estate of Norman Rockwell, reprinted by permission of the Estate of Norman Rockwell. Photo courtesy of The Norman Rockwell Museum at Stockbridge, MA.

Norman Rockwell Postcard Book © 1987 by Running Press Book Publishers

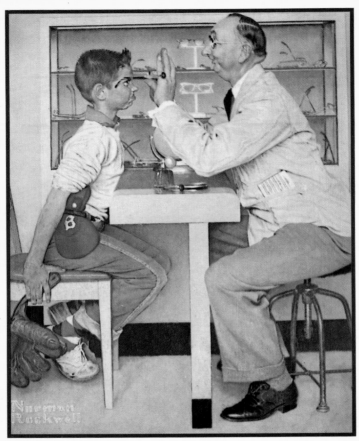

Norman Rockwell

The Optician

Family Tree by Norman Rockwell. Cover for *The Saturday Evening Post*, October 24, 1959. "I had the most trouble with the pirate at the bottom of the tree...Most of the difficulty sprang from my reluctance to begin the family with such a disreputable, fierce, coarse character." —Norman Rockwell. Collection of The Norman Rockwell Museum at Stockbridge, MA. Copyright © 1959 Estate of Norman Rockwell, reproduced by permission.

Norman Rockwell Postcard Book © 1987 by Running Press Book Publishers

Norman Rockwell

Family Tree

The Marriage License by Norman Rockwell. Cover for *The Saturday Evening Post*, June 11, 1955. "While I posed the young couple, Mr. Braman...was sitting just as I have painted him...I realized immediately that it was a far better pose than the one I had sketched. That proved to be the key to the cover." —Norman Rockwell. Collection of The Norman Rockwell Museum at Stockbridge, MA. Copyright © 1955 Estate of Norman Rockwell, reproduced by permission.

Norman Rockwell Postcard Book © 1987 by Running Press Book Publishers

Norman Rockwell

The Marriage License

Doctor and Doll by Norman Rockwell. Cover for *The Saturday Evening Post*, March 9, 1929. "Pop Fredericks...posed for the doctor...I used him as a model for (among others) a thug, Mr. Pickwick, Benjamin Franklin, a cellist, Santa Claus..." —Norman Rockwell. Copyright © 1929 Estate of Norman Rockwell, reprinted by permission of the Estate of Norman Rockwell. Photo courtesy of The Norman Rockwell Museum at Stockbridge, MA.

Norman Rockwell Postcard Book © 1987 by Running Press Book Publishers

Norman Rockwell

Doctor and Doll

Lion and Zookeeper by Norman Rockwell. Cover for *The Saturday Evening Post*, January 9, 1954. "At the sight and smell of the keeper's overflowing sandwich...the proud king of beasts becomes just a sad and hungry cat. I usually try to make a cover mean something more than just a gag." —Norman Rockwell. Copyright © 1954 Estate of Norman Rockwell, reprinted by permission of the Estate of Norman Rockwell. Photo courtesy of The Norman Rockwell Museum at Stockbridge, MA.

Norman Rockwell

Lion and Zookeeper

The Connoisseur by Norman Rockwell. Cover for *The Saturday Evening Post*, January 13, 1962. "...when I heard of a craze or a fad or anything which everyone was talking about, I'd do a cover of it..." —Norman Rockwell. Copyright © 1962 Estate of Norman Rockwell, reprinted by permission of the Estate of Norman Rockwell. Photo courtesy of The Norman Rockwell Museum at Stockbridge, MA.

Norman Rockwell Postcard Book © 1987 by Running Press Book Publishers

Norman Rockwell

The Connoisseur

The Rockwell family moved to Stockbridge, Massachusetts, in 1953, where the artist converted an old carriage house into a studio. There he continued to paint with great enthusiasm and success until his death in 1978.

For the many Americans who recognize themselves in these closely observed moments of American life, Rockwell's paintings have come to represent a collective family album.

With his affectionate portrayals of ordinary Americans, conceived with heartfelt good humor and painted in an almost photographically realistic style, Norman Rockwell recorded the everyday life of our nation for more than sixty years.

In 1916, when he was 21, he was working as an illustrator for children's magazines in New Rochelle, New York. That year he traveled to Philadelphia to offer three of his illustrations to the nation's largest mass-circulation magazine, *The Saturday Evening Post*. The art editor, to his credit, immediately recognized Rockwell's talent, accepted the three illustrations as covers for the *Post*, and asked for more. Thus began the long and happy association between Rockwell and the *Post*, for which Rockwell painted more than 300 covers.

Rockwell met and married Mary Barstow in 1930, and the couple had three sons. In 1939 the family moved to Arlington, Vermont, where Rockwell found inspiration for his work and discovered many of his neighbors to be "exactly the models I need for my purpose—the sincere, honest, homespun types that I love to paint."

When his studio burned to the ground in 1943, many of Rockwell's paintings were destroyed. The only record available today of many of Rockwell's works—including some reproduced in this book— are the *Post* covers themselves.